GROWTH
GUIDES
for Adults

Growing
Experience the Dynamic Path to Transformation

JOSH McDOWELL
SEAN McDOWELL

HARVEST HOUSE PUBLISHERS

EUGENE, OREGON

Cover by Koechel Peterson & Associates, Inc., Minneapolis, Minnesota

Cover photo © iStockphoto / Thinkstock

THE UNSHAKABLE TRUTH is a trademark of The Hawkins Children's LLC. Harvest House Publishers, Inc., is the exclusive licensee of the federally registered trademark THE UNSHAKABLE TRUTH.

GROWING—EXPERIENCE THE DYNAMIC PATH TO TRANSFORMATION
Course 7 of The Unshakable Truth® Journey Growth Guides
Copyright © 2012 by Josh McDowell Ministry and Sean McDowell
Published by Harvest House Publishers
Eugene, Oregon 97402
www.harvesthousepublishers.com

ISBN 978-0-7369-4646-9 (pbk.)
ISBN 978-0-7369-4647-6 (eBook)

Printed in the United States of America

12 13 14 15 16 17 18 19 20 / VP-NI / 10 9 8 7 6 5 4 3 2 1

CONTENTS

About the Authors

Authors Josh and Sean McDowell collaborated with their writer to bring you this Unshakable Truth Journey course. The content is based upon Scripture and the McDowells' book *The Unshakable Truth*.

Over 50-plus years, **Josh McDowell** has spoken to more than 10 million people in 120 countries about the evidence for Christianity and the difference the Christian faith makes in the world. He has authored or coauthored more than 120 books (with more than 51 million copies in print), including such classics as *More Than a Carpenter* and *New Evidence That Demands a Verdict*.

Sean McDowell is an educator and a popular speaker at schools, churches, and conferences nationwide. He is author of *Ethix: Being Bold in a Whatever World*, coauthor of *Understanding Intelligent Design*, and general editor of *Apologetics for a New Generation* and *The Apologetics Study Bible for Students*. He is currently pursuing a PhD in apologetics and worldview studies. Sean's website, www.seanmcdowell.org, offers his blog, many articles and videos, and much additional curriculum.

About the Writer

Dave Bellis is a ministry consultant focusing on ministry planning and product development. He is a writer, producer, and product developer. He and his wife, Becky, have two grown children and live in northeastern Ohio.

Acknowledgments

We would like to thank the many people who brought creativity and insight to forming this course:

Terri Snead and David Ferguson of Great Commandment Network for their writing insights for the TruthTalk and Truth Encounter sections of this growth guide.

Terry Glaspey for his insights and guidance as he helped in the development of the Unshakable Truth Journey concept.

Paul Gossard for his skillful editing of this manuscript.

And finally, the entire team at Harvest House, who graciously endured the process with us.

Josh McDowell
Sean McDowell
Dave Bellis

WHAT IS THE UNSHAKABLE TRUTH JOURNEY ALL ABOUT?

You hear people talk about having a personal relationship with God and knowing Christ. But what does that really mean? Sure, they probably are saying they are a Christian and God has personally forgiven them of their sins. But is that all of what being a Christian really is—being a person forgiven by God?

We are here to say that being a follower of Christ is much, much more than that. Everything you are and what you are becoming as a person is wrapped up in it. When Jesus said he was "the way, the truth, and the life" (John 14:6) he was offering us a supernatural way to follow in his way, his truth, and his life. As we do, we begin to understand what we were meant to know and be and how we were meant to live. Actually, when we become a follower of Christ we begin to take on Jesus' view of the world and begin to think like and be motivated like and live like Christ. And that brings incredible joy and satisfaction to life.

So when we see life and relationships as Jesus sees them, we begin to get a clear picture of who we are and discover our true identity. We begin to realize why we are here and recognize our purpose and meaning in life. We begin to know where we are going and experience our destiny and mission in a life larger than ourselves. Being a Christian—a committed follower of Christ—unlocks our identity, purpose, and destiny in life. It is then that the natural process of spiritual reproduction takes place. That is when imparting the faith to our family and others around us becomes a reality. But what is involved in being that kind of a follower of Christ—a person who has joy and satisfaction in life and knows how to effectively impart the faith to the next generation?

The Unshakable Truth Journey gets to the core of what being a true follower of Christ means and what knowing Christ is all about. Together you and your group will begin a journey that will last a lifetime. It is a journey into what you as a follower of Christ are to believe biblically, how you process your beliefs into core values, and how you live them out in all your relationships. In fact, we will take the core truths of Christianity and break them down into a five-step process:

1. *What truths do you as a Christian believe biblically?*

   In the first step you and your group will interact with what we as Christians believe about God, his Word, and so on.

2. *Why do you believe those truths?*

   Sure, you can say you believe certain truths because they are biblical, but when you know *why* they are true it grounds you in your faith. Additionally, it gives you confidence to pass them on to others—especially your family.

3. *How are these truths relevant to life?*

   In many respects truth isn't very meaningful until you see how it is relevant to your own life.

4. *How do you live these truths out personally?*

   Knowing how the truth of Christianity is relevant is necessary, but what it leads to is understanding how that truth is to become a living reality in your own life. That's where the rubber meets the road, so to speak.

5. *How do you, as a group, live these truths out before your community and world?*

   As Christians we are all to be "salt" and "light" to

the world around us. In this step you and your group will discover how to impact your own community with truth that is lived out corporately—as a body.

Be warned! The Unshakable Truth Journey isn't a program to study what Christianity is all about. Simply discovering what something is about has great limitations and ends up being of little value. Rather, this journey is about experiencing firsthand how God's truth is to be experienced in your life right now and, in fact, for the rest of your life. It's about knowing God's truth in a real, experiential way. The apostle John said, "It is by our actions that we know we are living in the truth" (1 John 3:19). You will be challenged repeatedly to increasingly know certain truths by experiencing them continually in your relationship with God and with those around you. It is then you will be able to pass on this ever-increasing faith journey to your family and friends.

There will be two specific exercises that appear throughout these courses. The first is entitled "Truth Encounter." This section is an invitation for you to stop and carefully reflect on the truth of each session. You'll be asked to encounter a truth of God as you relate personally with Jesus, as you live out the truth of God's Word with your small group, or as you relate personally with his people. Please don't rush past these Truth Encounters. They are designed to equip you in how to experience truth right in the room you're in!

The second exercise is an assignment for the week, called "TruthTalk." The TruthTalks are designed as conversation starters—ways to engage others in spiritual discussions. They will create opportunities for you to share what you've experienced in this course with others around you. This will help you communicate God's truth with others as you share vulnerably about your own Unshakable Truth Journey.

What you discover here is to last a lifetime and beyond. You will never finish in this life nor in the life to come. God's truths are designed to be enjoyed forever. You see, experiencing God's truth and knowing him will grow throughout eternity, and your love of him will expand to contain it. And that process begins in the here and now. Your relationship with God may have begun 5 months, 5 years, or 50 years ago—it doesn't matter. The truths explored in these courses are to be applied at every level of life. And what is so encouraging is that while these truths are eternally deep they can be embraced and experienced by even a young child. That is the beauty and mystery of God's truth!

This particular Unshakable Truth Journey is one of 12 different growth guides. All the growth guides are based upon Josh and Sean McDowell's book *The Unshakable Truth,* which is the companion book to this course. The book covers 12 core truths of the Christian faith.

The growth guide you have in your hand covers the truth about a transformed life in Christ. Your transformed life in Christ defines why you are here on earth. These five sessions explore how you can grow in Christ and how living Christlike gives you your sense of purpose. Check out the other Unshakable Truth Journey courses in the back of this book.

Okay then, let our journey begin.

UNDERSTANDING YOUR PURPOSE

Have you ever bought something that needed to be put together, and you either lost the instruction booklet or it came without one? Was it challenging, frustrating, or what? Share your experience.

_____

_____

_____

_____

_____

Without an instruction booklet from the designer or creator of something it is often difficult to determine how that something is supposed to work or why it was designed that way in the first place. The same goes for human beings. In many respects humans have lost touch with the original Designer/Creator. If you were to write an instruction booklet for the human race, what would you say they were designed to be or do? In other words, what would you say is our purpose in life? Discuss.

_____

_____

_____

_____

_____

_____

_____

OUR GROUP OBJECTIVE

To discover through Scripture
our purpose for living—
why we are here.

Someone read Genesis 1:26.

What was the created design of humans? What or who were humans originally modeled after?

_____

_____

What are some characteristics of that original design—God's image and likeness? (This doesn't mean God's infinite powers and characteristics, but his relational image.)

_____

_____

_____

_____

_____

If you were to sum up God's relational image in one core quality and put a name to it, what would that word be? Someone read 1 John 4:7-8.

_____

_____

Based on 1 John 4:9-10, what did God's love do?

_____

_____

_____

_____

_____

Jesus described the quality or essence of this kind of love. Read Matthew 7:12 and then contrast that quality with that of Galatians 5:19-21.

What do you see as the primary difference between the two images? There are two distinct focuses here—what are they?

- The focus of Matthew 7:12 is on

    _____

- The focus of Galatians 5:19-21 is on

_____

Someone read the following aloud.

> The primary relational characteristic of God is a
> love that gives and sacrifices for another. It is a love
> that looks out for the best interest of another. It
> is a love that is "patient and kind...not jealous or
> boastful or proud or rude...does not demand its
> own way" (1 Corinthians 13:4-5). This relational
> characteristic of God's image is not self-centered; it
> is other-focused.
>
> But because humans have sinned and have been
> separated from God they have lost the true rela-
> tional image of God. We, as the human race, have
> become a people whose "god is their appetite, they
> brag about shameful things, and all they think
> about is this life here on earth" (Philippians 3:19).
> And with the loss of God's relational image and
> likeness we are self-centered and unable to fulfill
> our original design and purpose.

Someone read Ephesians 4:17-24.

Based on this passage, do you want to alter any of your answers to the question "What is your purpose in life?"

_____
_____
_____
_____
_____

Created in God's relational image, we were to join in the God-head's perfect circle of love and enjoy all the benefits of being one with him and one with each other. But sin changed all that. Human nature was contaminated by sin and self-centeredness. Yet God's plan is to transform our human nature back into his divine nature.

Someone read Romans 8:29, 2 Corinthians 3:18, and 2 Peter 1:3-4.

Our lives as a Christian are to look like, talk like, and be motivated like who? _____

God gets something out of our living and being like him. What do you get out of your children following in your footsteps and living a life of integrity and godliness?

_____
_____
_____
_____
_____

Someone read 1 Corinthians 10:31.

So what does God get out of us being conformed to the image of his Son?

_____

_____

_____

_____

_____

Someone read the following. (This is drawn from chapter 28 of *The Unshakable Truth* book.)

"God loved us and chose us in Christ to be holy and without fault in his eyes. His unchanging plan has always been to adopt us into his own family by bringing us to himself through Jesus Christ. And this gave him great pleasure" (Ephesians 1:4-5). What does it do for God when we begin conforming to his Son's image? It gives him pleasure. It honors him. It glorifies his name and image. And that defines our very purpose in life. That is why we are here—to honor God and give him glory and joy.

There is nothing self-centered about God creating us in order to bring him honor and joy. Because bringing God honor through living and relating as he does is what gives us joy too. Acting according to God's ways brings blessing because all that is defined as perfectly right and good is derived from his nature—the very nature we are empowered to live out. (See James 1:17.)

Therefore:

> **We believe the truth that followers of Christ are meant to live in relationship with God and be transformed into the likeness of Christ, which defines our very purpose for living— to honor and glorify God.**

We were created to live contented lives of joy. We were made to know the gratifying joy of being accepted, approved of, and appreciated, with the ability to freely love and be loved. We were designed to experience fulfillment and satisfaction beyond measure, contentment and peace beyond understanding, and complete joy. And that kind of meaningful life comes only from living in fellowship with God and being conformed to his image. When we come into relationship with him, it begins a process of change that allows his divine nature to permeate our lives. And as we live out that Godlike nature we fulfill the very reason we are here.

Truth Encounter

Someone read the following.

The apostle Paul talks about transformed followers of Christ who "have stripped off your old evil nature and all its wicked deeds. In its place you have clothed yourselves with a brand-new nature that is continually being renewed as you learn more and more about Christ, who created this new nature within you" (Colossians 3:9-10).

Let's encounter the truth of what some of these new clothes are that we are to wear. Verses 12-14 of Colossians 3 identify seven Christlike characteristics referred to as clothing. What are they, and how are we to live them out with our family and friends?

Paul said, "Since God chose you to be the holy people whom he loves, you must clothe yourself with...

1. _____ (first characteristic in Colossians 3:12-14).

"A specific example of how I can live this characteristic out with my family is _____

_____

_____

_____."

Share your example with the group.

2. _____ (second characteristic in Colossians 3:12-14).

"A specific example of how I can live this characteristic out with my family is _____

_____

_____

_____."

Share your example with the group.

3. _____ (third characteristic in Colossians 3:12-14).

"A specific example of how I can live this characteristic out with my family is _____

_____

_____

_____."

Share your example with the group.

4. _____ (fourth characteristic in Colossians 3:12-14).

"A specific example of how I can live this characteristic out with my family is _____

_____

_____

_____."

Share your example with the group.

5. _____ (fifth characteristic in Colossians 3:12-14).

"A specific example of how I can live this characteristic out with my family is _____

_____

_____

_____."

Share your example with the group.

6. _____ (sixth characteristic in Colossians 3:12-14).

"A specific example of how I can live this characteristic out with my family is _____

_____

_____

_____."

Share your example with the group.

7. _____ (seventh characteristic in Colossians 3:12-14).

"A specific example of how I can live this characteristic out with my family is _____

_____

_____

_____."

Share your example with the group.

Take time to pray together now that the characteristics above will become a living reality in your life as you are conformed more and more to the likeness of Christ through the power of his Holy Spirit.

Truth Talk—An Assignment of the Week

This week take time to share one of the seven characteristics of Christ in Colossians 3:12-14 with a family member or friend. Let them know you are asking God to reflect that Christlike image in and through your life to them. Consider saying something like:

Our purpose in life is to honor our Creator God by

1 "I have been asking God lately to reflect his characteristic of _____ in my life (kindness, humility, forgiveness, living in relationship with him and out of that relationship becoming more and more like him. God created us to bring glory to himself. And we glorify God—reflect honorably upon him—as we live in devoted love of him, desiring to please him. "Whatever you eat or drink or whatever you do," Paul said, "you must do all for the glory of God" (1 Corinthians 10:31).

or whatever you choose from verses 12-14). I know I haven't always been that to you. But I want to. I sense that would look like…

_____

_____

_____

_____."

2 "In my small group I have been identifying various qualities of Christ's image. Can I share with you one I'd like to emulate more? It is (share your example)…

_____

_____

_____

_____."

Read chapter 28 of *The Unshakable Truth* book as a review of this session and chapter 29 to prepare for next week's session.

||||||||||||||||||||||||||||||||||||||||||||||||||||||||||||||||||||||||||||||||||

Close in Prayer

EVIDENCE OF A CHANGED LIFE

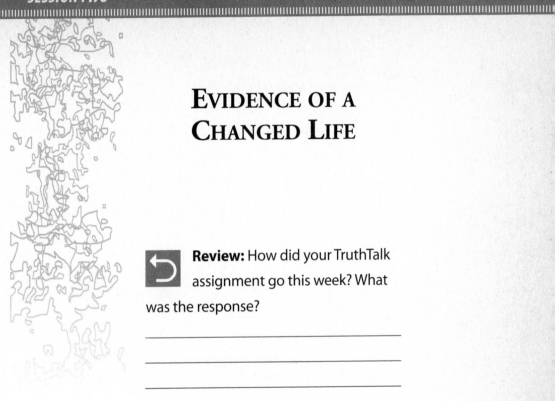

Review: How did your TruthTalk assignment go this week? What was the response?

_____

_____

_____

_____

_____

When you were growing up, did you sometimes struggle because you observed the lives of hypocrites? Did it bother you that some people said they believed certain things but didn't live them out? Share your experience.

_____

_____

_____

_____

_____

Someone read Matthew 7:15-17.

We are not to judge the hearts and motives of others. But based on these verses, what is one way a person can tell if another is living out Christlikeness?

_____

_____

_____

_____

_____

OUR GROUP OBJECTIVE

To explore what the transforming power of God does to a life and how it has changed our own lives.

Someone read John 3:3-8 and 2 Corinthians 5:14-17.

For a person to be "born again" or to receive a "new life" it requires a supernatural transformation by God. What are some changes that commonly take place in a person who has been

born of God? Brainstorm together what those changes include.
(If you need further help from Scripture see Galatians 5:19-26.)

_____

_____

_____

_____

_____

_____

_____

Let's be specific and personal. What changes have you realized
in your own life? Contrast your life before Christ and your life in
Christ. Then share them with the group.

"Before Christ I had these desires and I acted this way:

_____

_____

_____

_____

_____

_____

_____."

"God transformed me into his child, and now I have these
desires and I try to act this way:

_____

_____

_____

_____

_____

_____

_____."

Becoming a transformed follower of Christ changes us from the inside out. But does that change stop at some point, or is it ongoing? _____

_____

_____

Someone read Philippians 3:12.

How did Paul characterize his changed life in Christ? Had he arrived, was he still in process, or what?

_____

_____

_____

_____

What attitude of the heart should an imperfect yet godly person possess?

Read Psalm 51:16-17.

_____

_____

_____

_____

_____

We are not always perfect representations of the truth, nor do we reflect Christlikeness at all times. But can God still use those times as "teachable moments" for our children and families? How?

_____

_____

_____

_____

_____

_____

Someone read the following. (This is drawn from chapter 3 of *The Unshakable Truth* book.)

> Josh and Sean share an example out of their own lives that illustrates how God can use our failures to teach our children.
>
> Lest you give up hope before you even begin, let us be quick to say that being a representation of the truth doesn't mean we must live perfect lives. I (Sean) remember a time when I was still living with my parents, and my dad was in a heated argument

with Mom. To be honest, Dad was being pretty awful. At one point in the argument he threw a folder down on the table and said, "I'm out of here." He stormed out the door and drove off. I remember thinking, *Man, is he ever ticked*.

I, along with my sisters, went back to doing whatever we had been doing prior to the "Josh explosion." But it wasn't long before Dad was back and called us all in for a meeting. In front of us all he told my mom how wrong he had been and how sorry he was that he had hurt her, and he sought her forgiveness. He turned to each of us kids and told us how disrespectful he had been to our mother, and he sought our forgiveness too. Now, my dad's earlier actions were far from a perfect model of Christlikeness, but he was, nonetheless, a great model of one who was truly following Christ. How? When he realized his offense and sought forgiveness, he was being sensitive to the convicting Spirit of God. My dad was a model of a person who sincerely desires to be conformed to the image of Christ.

Believe it or not, those around us need to see us fail and humbly seek forgiveness. The Spirit of truth through his Word is there "to make us realize what is wrong in our lives. It straightens us out and teaches us to do what is right" (2 Timothy 3:16).

Being a living reflection of the truth in a fallen world means we sometimes mess up, but when we do we must realize it and make amends. The great and spiritual apostle Paul said, "I don't mean to say that I have already achieved these things or that I have already reached perfection! But I keep working toward that day when I will finally be all that Christ Jesus saved me for and wants me to be" (Philippians 3:12).

||||||||||||||||||||||||||||||||||||||||||||||||||||||||||||||||||||||||||||||||||

Truth Encounter

Someone read Hebrews 12:1-2.

As we live a life of faith, what is it that we are to "throw off" or "strip off"?

_____

_____

_____

We all seem to have a hindrance or sin that easily slows down our progress toward Christlikeness. But how do we run this Christian race with endurance? Where do we keep our focus? (See verse 2.)

_____

_____

How does that focus help us live the Christian life?

_____

_____

_____

_____

_____

Let's experience James 5:16 together. Someone read that passage.

What does confessing our weaknesses and those things that hinder our progress toward Christlikeness do for us? What are the benefits of confessing to one another?

_____

_____

_____

_____

_____

What are some downsides to confessing to one another? In other words, what is some negative fallout that could happen when others hear you confessing your weaknesses?

_____

_____

_____

_____

_____

Therefore to avoid those downsides, what atmosphere is condu-
cive to confession and how must you and your group exhibit it?

_____

_____

_____

_____

_____

Healthy confession needs a safe place, a nonjudgmental place,
a place where understanding, supportive, and empathetic people will hold your confession in confidence and in prayer. If that
kind of place or people exists, confessing your faults one to
another can be very rewarding.

Someone read Psalm 139:23-24.

Why would you want God to search your heart and point out
anything that offends him? What benefit is there to being vul-
nerable to God in that way?

_____

_____

_____

_____

_____

With a heart open and transparent to God, share areas of
your life that especially need God's grace—areas you want to

strengthen in order to reflect honorably upon God. (*Note*: Share wisely. Avoid any area that would implicate any other person. Restrict your confession to what you struggle with and where you sense you need help and strength.)

_____

_____

_____

_____

_____

_____

Take time and pray together to first ask God for his power and strength to live more like him. Then thank him for his grace and transforming power, which is continually changing your life.

TruthTalk—An Assignment of the Week

This week take time with a family member or friend to share an area of weakness that you are asking God to strengthen. Consider saying something like:

Multiplied millions of lives over the course of history speak out as a testimony to the God of redemption who changes lives. There are not enough books to hold the stories. If you have placed your faith in Christ, you are living proof that a "metamorphosis" has taken place—you, a child of God, have been redeemed and are being continually transformed into the image of Christ... Whenever you have an opportunity to tell others how God has changed you, take it.

1 "Recently I've been asking God to search my thoughts and motives and reveal anything that hinders me from being like him. And I've come to realize I struggle in this area of my life that...

_____
_____
_____
_____."

2 "The Christian life is a process of becoming more like Jesus. And there have been times I've been unlike him and I know I have hurt you. Would you please forgive me for when I recently...

_____
_____
_____
_____."

3 "I've been asking God to search my heart and help me to be more like him. And even though I love you, I know I have at times been

_____.

Will you share with me now a time when I have hurt you so I can specifically ask your forgiveness?"

Read chapter 30 of *The Unshakable Truth* book.

||||||||||||||||||||||||||||||||||||||||||||||||||||||||||||||||||||||||||||||||||||||||||||||

Close in Prayer

WHO IS THE TRANSFORMED YOU?

Review: How did your TruthTalk assignment go this week? What was the response?

_____

_____

_____

_____

_____

Oftentimes kids are teased as they grow up. Did you ever experience a time when one of your peers or even an adult put you down and said mean or cruel things about you? How did it affect you? Do you still feel the effects of that today? If so, how?

_____

_____

_____

_____

_____

_____

_____

The experiences of our past have largely determined how we view ourselves—our self-concept or self-image. Do you have a healthy self-concept? Do you see the positive healthy traits of yourself as well as the negative side that isn't so healthy, and do you then love and accept yourself for who you are? Or do you tend to put yourself down (engage in self-condemnation) and sometimes become your worst critic? Explain.

_____

_____

_____

_____

_____

OUR GROUP OBJECTIVE

To discover how God sees the transformed you and take positive steps to see yourself as he sees you.

Someone read Romans 8:1.

If a person is transformed into God's child and is under no

condemnation, why do you think Christians struggle with self-condemnation?

_____

_____

_____

_____

_____

_____

Someone read Romans 12:2, Colossians 3:9-10, and Philippians 1:6.

When a person experiences a transformed relationship with God, what is changed instantly, and what changes progressively?

_____

_____

_____

_____

_____

_____

Someone read the following. (This is drawn from chapter 30 of *The Unshakable Truth* book.)

> Following Christ is a process, and that process involves an ever-increasing change into Christlikeness. Notice how Paul refers to the process when he

concludes that your brand-new nature "is continually being renewed as you learn more and more about Christ, who created this new nature within you" (Colossians 3:9-10).

That renewal has begun within us, but it must be continued day in and day out as Christ's relational nature is unleashed through every aspect of our attitudes and actions. Peter said, "By his divine power, God has given us everything we need for living a godly life" (2 Peter 1:3 NLT).

There is a very important principle here about the transformation process of becoming more and more like Christ. As followers of Christ we *do* live differently from our old lives. But the doing isn't what continually transforms us. It is living in relationship with Christ and his nature, which is being imparted and empowered by the Holy Spirit, that continually transforms us. *So the process isn't so much in learning to do all the right things perfectly as it is learning who Christ is and acting according to his new nature within us.*

There are certain things that are true of you from the moment you trust Christ as Savior and Lord. God sees you differently because he has raised you to new life in relationship to him. The truest statements about the transformed you are what God

says about you in his Word. If what you think and
feel about yourself does not line up with how God
describes you, you are making yourself the victim
of a mistaken identity.

It has been said that *our self-concept is largely determined by
what we believe the most important person in our lives thinks
about us.*

Your parents were very important to you when you were
young. Think back on what your parents repeatedly said about
you. Did you believe them, and did that become part of your
self-concept? What was it they repeatedly said, and is it part of
your self-concept even today? Explain.

_____

_____

_____

_____

_____

_____

Is Jesus a very important person in your life? What does he have
to say about you? Someone read the passages below, and as
a group fill in the blanks that represent your godly description
and position in Christ.

- Ephesians 1:3—"I am blessed with _____
  _____."

- Ephesians 1:4—"I was chosen before _____
  to be _____."

- Ephesians 1:5—"I was chosen to be _____
  _____."

- Ephesians 1:7—"I have _____."

- Ephesians 1:11—"I have received _____
  _____."

- Ephesians 1:13—"I am identified as God's own by
  receiving _____."

Someone read the following.

> Do you believe what the most important person
> in your life believes about you? Paul prayed for all
> followers of Christ when he said, "I pray that your
> hearts will be flooded with light so that you can
> understand the wonderful future he has promised
> to those he called. I want you to realize what a rich
> and glorious inheritance he has given his people. I
> pray that you will begin to understand the incred-
> ible greatness of his power for us who believe in
> him" (Ephesians 1:18-19).

Truth Encounter

There are many other things God says about you that are true. Allow what he says to penetrate your thinking and your life—allow them to become part of your self-concept.

Someone read aloud what God says about you in seven areas below. Then express to the group how you might view yourself differently and behave differently as you encounter and act upon these truths.

These are phrased as if God is speaking directly to you.

- "You are my very own child" (from John 1:12). How do you respond to God's view of you as his very own child?

  _____

  _____

  _____

  _____

  _____

- "I live in you through my Holy Spirit" (from 1 Corinthians 3:16). How do you respond to God, who has taken up residence in you?

  _____

_____

_____

_____

_____

- "You have ready access to my wisdom" (from James 1:5). How do you respond to God's invitation to tap into his wisdom?

  _____

  _____

  _____

  _____

  _____

- "I freely forgive you and do not condemn you at all" (from Romans 8:1 and Colossians 1:14). How do you respond to God's unconditional acceptance of you?

  _____

  _____

  _____

  _____

  _____

- "I tenderly love you and you are my dearest friend" (from Jeremiah 31:3 and John 15:15). How do you respond to God, who sees you as his dearest friend?

  _____

  _____

_____

_____

_____

- "I have given you eternal life because I want you to live with me forever" (from John 10:28). How do you respond to God's wanting you to be with him forever?

  _____

  _____

  _____

  _____

  _____

- "I will never let anything come between us—you are secure in my love" (from Romans 8:35-39 and 1 John 5:18). How do you respond to God's protection and a love that will not let you go?

  _____

  _____

  _____

  _____

  _____

Take time together now as a group to give praise to God through prayer and song. Thank him that he sees you as a transformed child in loving relationship with him. He cares for you. Tell him how much you care for him.

TruthTalk—An Assignment of the Week

Share with a family member or a friend how humbled you are that God views you as he does. Consider saying something like:

Studying the Bible, attending church, and sharing our faith do not cause God to regard us as more redeemed, justified, or sanctified, or more adopted as his child. He *already* sees us in these ways because they define who we really are. So we don't *do* our way into becoming God's adopted children; we don't *do* things to cause his divine nature to dwell within us. We are not changed

1 "I have been discovering from Scripture what God thinks of me and it causes me to be so grateful and humbled. Can I tell you what I'm learning God says about me? He says I'm his very own child, that I'm…

_____

_____

_____

_____."

2 "I've been learning lately that I haven't had as healthy a self-concept as I should. That has been because…

_____

_____

_____

_____."

from the outside in; we are changed from the inside out. As we live in relationship with Christ, we can start behaving according to our new nature and do those things that God's children do—act like Christ.

3 "I want you to have a healthy self-concept. Let me tell you how important you are to me…

_____

_____

_____

_____."

Read chapter 31 of *The Unshakable Truth* book.

Close in Prayer

WHAT A TRANSFORMED LIFE LOOKS LIKE

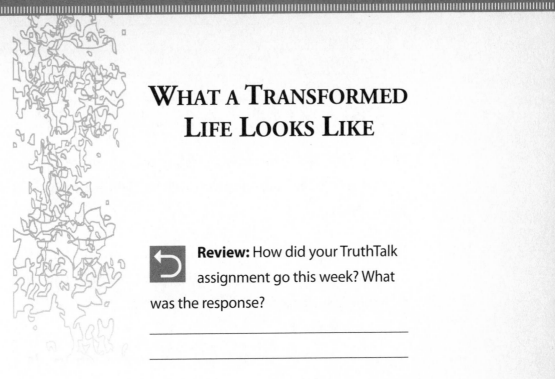

Review: How did your TruthTalk assignment go this week? What was the response?

_____

_____

_____

_____

_____

Marriage is the relational union of a man and a woman. It represents a commitment of two people to love each other "till death do us part."

Take a few moments to describe what the loving marital relationship is supposed to look like. When marriage is lived out as it should be, what does it look like?

_____

_____

_____

_____

_____

_____

_____

When we become transformed children of God, we are brought into the relational union with the Godhead. Someone read John 17:16-21.

Jesus' prayer for us is to be one with him and the Father and the Spirit. Based on this passage, describe what that loving godly relationship is supposed to look like. When oneness in God is lived out it looks like…

_____

_____

_____

_____

_____

_____

OUR GROUP OBJECTIVE

To define Godlike love and describe what it looks like in our lives.

In a previous session we discovered that God is love and in his love he sacrifices and gives to us—godly love is not self-centered, but other-focused.

Someone read Matthew 7:12 and Matthew 22:37-39.

Can you have a love that is other-focused yet love yourself? How can a Godlike love focus on others while at the same time loving self? Explain.

_____

_____

_____

_____

_____

Someone read Ephesians 5:25-29.

Based on this passage, what does a proper love of self look like? What does this kind of love look like in a marriage relationship?

_____

_____

_____

_____

_____

Then how would you define Godlike love?

_____

_____

_____

_____

_____

_____

Someone read the following. (This is drawn from chapter 31 of *The Unshakable Truth* book.)

> A lot of people know that God is love and that we are to love others as he does, but they lack a concise definition as to what Godlike love is. In 1 Corinthians, the apostle Paul gives a good description of what love does and does not do. "Love is patient and kind. Love is *not jealous* or *boastful* or *proud* or *rude.* Love does not demand its own way. Love is not irritable, and it keeps no record of when it has been wronged. It is never glad about injustice but rejoices whenever the truth wins out" (1 Corinthians 13:4-6).
>
> Paul also wrote that "love does no wrong to anyone" (Romans 13:10). Instead, we are to treat all people as we would like to be treated. Paul put it this way: "Each of you should look not only to your own interests, but also to the interests of others" (Philippians 2:4 NIV).
>
> When Jesus was asked to identify the most

important commandment, he said it was to love God and "love your neighbor as yourself" (Matthew 22:39). Paul gave us a specific application of this principle when he told husbands "to love their wives as they love their own bodies…No one hates his own body but lovingly cares for it" (Ephesians 5:28-29). Loving like this is one way of living out the holiness of God.

Drawing from these verses and others similar, we can derive a concise definition of pure Godlike love. *Love is making the security, happiness, and welfare of another person as important as your own.* This is Godlike love, a pure love that protects the loved one from harm and provides for his or her good. Godlike love is giving and trusting, unselfish and sacrificial, secure and safe, loyal and forever. And because its priority is to protect and provide for the loved one, Godlike love will not do things that are harmful to the security, happiness, and welfare of another person.

Write out the above definition of a Godlike love:

"Love is making _____

_____

_____

_____."

Someone read John 13:34-35.

How are we to love? _____

Give a few examples of how the nature of Jesus' love made the security, happiness, and welfare of others as important as his own. (For example, "Jesus' love forgives others," "Jesus' love feeds others," and so on.)

- Jesus' love _____.

- Jesus' love _____.

- Jesus' love _____.

Someone read the following.

> Following Jesus' death and resurrection, God in-spired the disciples and apostles to write out spe-cific instructions to show what Christlike love looks like in our lives. Many of these instructions appear in the "one another" passages of Scripture. At least 35 times in the New Testament, we see a recurring word pattern—an action verb followed by the words "one another." These admonitions give us practical examples of how to love as Jesus loved. We know, for example, the nature of Jesus' love was gentle, humble, and forgiving. Scripture admonishes us to live out those characteristics of

Christ by being gentle to one another (Ephesians
4:2), being humble toward one another (1 Peter
5:5), and forgiving one another (Colossians 3:13).
By identifying these "one another" passages, we get
a much clearer picture of how Christ wants us to
live out his divine nature of love in our lives.

Someone read the following scriptures and identify the "one anothers" that show how we are to love each other as Jesus loves us.

- _____ one another (Romans 15:7).

- _____ one another (Colossians 3:13).

- _____ one another (1 Thessalonians 5:11).

Consider the other "one anothers" of Christlike love.

- Be gentle to one another (Ephesians 4:2).

- Be clothed in humility toward one another (1 Peter 5:5).

- Weep with one another (Romans 12:15).

- Live in harmony with one another (Romans 12:16).

- Don't judge one another (Romans 14:13).

- Be patient with one another (Ephesians 4:2).

- Admonish one another (Colossians 3:16).

- Greet one another (Romans 16:16).

- Wait for one another (1 Corinthians 11:33).

- Care for one another (1 Corinthians 12:25).

- Serve one another (Galatians 5:13).

- Be kind to one another (Ephesians 4:32).

- Be devoted to one another (Romans 12:10).

- Be compassionate toward one another (Ephesians 4:32).

- Submit to one another (Ephesians 5:21).

- Make allowances for one another (Colossians 3:13).

- Stimulate love in one another (Hebrews 10:24).

- Offer hospitality to one another (1 Peter 4:9).

- Minister gifts to one another (1 Peter 4:10).

- Rejoice with one another (Romans 12:15; 1 Corinthians 12:26).

- Don't slander one another (James 4:11).

- Don't grumble against one another (James 5:9).

- Confess your sins to one another (James 5:16).

- Pray for one another (James 5:16).

- Fellowship with one another (1 John 1:7).

- Don't be puffed up against one another
  (1 Corinthians 4:6).

- Carry one another's burdens (Galatians 6:2).

- Honor one another (Romans 12:10).

- Depend on one another (Romans 12:5 AMP)

- Prefer one another (Romans 12:10).

- Comfort one another (2 Corinthians 1:4).

||||||||||||||||||||||||||||||||||||||||||||||||||||||||||||||||||||||||||||||||||||||||||||||||||||

Truth Encounter

Someone read Ephesians 4:29.

There is power in your words. According to this passage what are your words to accomplish in another?

_____

_____

_____

_____

_____

_____

Someone read the following.

> In the New American Standard version the passage says that we are to use our words for "edification according to the need of the moment that it may give grace to those who hear" (Ephesians 4:29 NASB). Another translation says, "Let everything you say be good and helpful, so that your words will be an encouragement to those who hear them" (Ephesians 4:29 NLT). And in 1 Thessalonians 5:11 it says "encourage one another." Let's experience that Scripture verse together.

When does a person need encouragement? Identify some circumstances when words of encouragement meet the need of the moment.

_____

_____

_____

_____

_____

_____

Read the following.

> Encouragement is "the act of urging forward; positively persuading toward a goal; inspiring with courage, spirit or hope; stimulating towards a positive direction." The writer of the book of Hebrews challenges us to "consider how to stimulate one another to love and good deeds…encouraging one another" (Hebrews 10:24-25 NASB). Discouragement is a common affliction. We can feel discouraged when we lose sight of a goal. We can feel down when we experience rejection, failure, or when things don't work out as expected.

What does the need for encouragement sound like to you? Complete this sentence:

"When I feel discouraged or disappointed, I need to hear you

say _____

_____

_____."

Now share your sentence with the group.

What might encouraging words sound like? Brainstorm a couple of sentences that inspire hope and assure a person everything will work out. Come up with something that lets a person know you believe in them and that you are there for them.

_____

_____

_____

_____

_____

_____

_____

What might encouragement look like? Encouragement is conveyed by words, but it is also conveyed by actions, like a smile or a hug.

What are some other outward expressions of providing encouragement? Discuss and write them out here.

_____

_____

_____

_____

_____

_____

_____

Together, experience encouragement.

Someone (perhaps more than one) share a disappointment or frustrating situation you are going through right now. It may be a major disappointment or a minor discouragement. But share with the group the nature of your disappointment or discouragement.

_____

_____

_____

_____

_____

Now, others in the group offer words and expressions of encouragement in obedience to 1 Thessalonians 5:11.

Following this time, the person(s) being encouraged please answer this question: What is your heart's response to those around you right now?

_____

_____

_____

_____

_____

Thank God together in prayer that a loving God who encourages us has shared his love through his people.

TruthTalk—An Assignment of the Week

This week look for a time to be of encouragement to a family member or friend. Even if your loved one isn't particularly discouraged you can offer uplifting words that tell them they are important to you and that you believe in them. Consider saying something like:

Jesus had…taken on the role of a servant to wash the feet of his followers. And within that context he issues a new commandment: "A new command I give you: Love one another. As I have loved you, so you must love one another. By this all men will know that you are my disciples, if you love one another"(John 13:34-35 NIV)…

1 "You know, you put so much into (homework, a sport, a hobby, and so on) and sometimes it doesn't work out as you'd hoped. Yet you still keep trying. I want you to know that…

_____
_____
_____
_____."

2 "I know this is difficult for you. What can I do to help you accomplish your goals this week?"

_____
_____

This one command would be the mark of a true Christian. This "love one another as I have loved you" would be the universal identifier—the distinguishing brand—of Jesus' disciples. Loving as Christ loved would be a clear expression of God's holiness.

3 "I want to be an encouragement to you because you mean so much to me. How can I help you?"

_____

_____

_____

_____

_____

_____

Review chapter 31 of *The Unshakable Truth* book.

||||||||||||||||||||||||||||||||||||||||||||||||||||||||||||||||||||||||||||||||||||

Close in Prayer

LIVING OUT THE DEFINITION OF LOVE WITHIN YOUR COMMUNITY

Review: How did your TruthTalk assignment go this week? What was the response with those you shared?

_____

_____

_____

_____

_____

Someone read Philippians 2:14-15.

What kind of lives are we to live before the world?

_____

_____

_____

_____

_____

Look over the "one another" list from Session 4 or on pages 267–268 of *The Unshakable Truth* book. Pick four or five "one anothers" that you as a group could experience with people outside your group—expressions of a love that *"makes the security, happiness, and welfare of others as important as your own."*

_____

_____

_____

_____

_____

_____

Someone read the following.

> When you as a group love those in your community as Christ loves you, God is glorified because his presence and Spirit ministers through you to those in need.

OUR GROUP OBJECTIVE

To plan a group activity that involves loving others in your community who are in need of comfort, encouragement, or aid.

In this session you as a group are to brainstorm about an effort to reach out to people in the community to meet their emotional, relational, or physical needs. This could be to those who are without a job, suffering alone, rejected by others, and so on.

Brainstorm: _____

_____

_____

_____

_____

_____

_____

_____

_____

Take the time here to plan your project by doing the following:

Identify your activity: _____

_____

_____

_____

Set the date and time for your activity: _____

_____

_____

_____

Determine what is needed to execute your activity: _____

_____

_____

_____

Assign responsibilities and tasks for who will be doing what:

_____

_____

_____

_____

Have someone in your group track and record what is being done. This is to record the results of your efforts.

_____

_____

_____

Bring every aspect of your activity before the Lord in prayer.

Someone read Ephesians 5:1-2.

As you close in prayer, ask God that he would be honored and praised as you follow the example of Christ in how he loves you.

_____

_____

_____

_____

_____

||||||||||||||||||||||||||||||||||||||||||||||||||||||||||||||||||||||||||||||||||||||

Assignment of the Week

Execute your activity.

Take the Complete Unshakable Truth® Journey!

The Unshakable Truth Journey gets to the heart of what being a true follower of Christ means and what knowing him is all about. Each five-session course is based on one of 12 core truths of the Christian faith presented in Josh and Sean McDowell's book *The Unshakable Truth*®.

The Unshakable Truth Journey is uniquely positioned for today's culture because it 1) highlights how Christianity's beliefs affect relationships, 2) promotes a relational, group context in which Christians can experience the teaching in depth, and 3) shows believers how they can live out Christianity's central truths before their community and world.

More than just a program, The Unshakable Truth Journey is a tool for long-term change and transformation!

CREATED—EXPERIENCE YOUR UNIQUE PURPOSE is devoted to the truth that God is—he exists, and he created human beings for a reason. It lays a foundation for who people are because they're God's creation, who God designed them to be, and how they can live a life of fulfillment.

INSPIRED—EXPERIENCE THE POWER OF GOD'S WORD explores the truth that God has spoken and revealed himself to humanity within the Bible. Further, he gave us his Word for a very clear purpose—to provide for us and protect us.

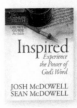

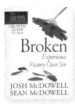

BROKEN—EXPERIENCE VICTORY OVER SIN examines the truth about humankind's brokenness because of original sin, humankind's ongoing problem with sin, and how instead to make right choices in life.

ACCEPTED—EXPERIENCE GOD'S UNCONDITIONAL LOVE opens up the truth about God's redemption plan. The truth that God became human establishes his unconditional acceptance of us, which defines our worth. God values us in spite of our sin. This is the basis on which we gain a high sense of worth.

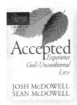

SACRIFICE—EXPERIENCE A DEEPER WAY TO LOVE digs into the truth about Christ's atonement. The truth that Christ had to die to purchase our salvation shows the true meaning of love—and how God can bring us into a right relationship with him in spite of our sin.

FORGIVEN—EXPERIENCE THE SURPRISING GRACE OF GOD explores the truth about the power of God's grace. The truth that God can offer us forgiveness in spite of our sin helps us understand how we actually obtain a relationship with him.

GROWING—EXPERIENCE THE DYNAMIC PATH TO TRANSFORMATION speaks to the truth about our transformed life in Christ. The truth about our transformed life in Christ defines who we are in this world and shows how we can know our purpose in life.

RESURRECTED—EXPERIENCE FREEDOM FROM THE FEAR OF DEATH focuses on the truth about Christ's resurrection. The truth that Christ rose from the grave and that his resurrection is a historical event assures us of eternal life and overcomes any fear of dying.

EMPOWERED—EXPERIENCE LIVING IN THE POWER OF THE SPIRIT covers the truth about the Trinity. The truth that God is three in one and defines how relationships work through the Holy Spirit lays the foundation for how we can experience the power of the Spirit.

PERSPECTIVE—EXPERIENCE THE WORLD THROUGH GOD'S EYES examines the truth about God's kingdom and how it defines a biblical worldview. These sessions show how to gain a biblical worldview.

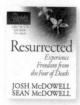

COMMUNITY—EXPERIENCE JESUS ALIVE IN HIS PEOPLE opens up the truth about the church. The truth about Christ's body—the church—provides us with our mission in life and shows us how to experience true community.

RESTORED—EXPERIENCE THE JOY OF YOUR DESTINY is devoted to the truth about the return of Christ. The truth that Jesus is coming back helps us grasp our destiny in life and gain an eternal perspective on life and death.

The Unshakable Truth Journey
Growing Growth Guide Evaluation Form

1. How many on average participated in your group? _____

2. Did you read all or a portion of *The Unshakable Truth* book? _____

3. Did your group leader use visual illustrations during this course? _____

4. *Group leader:* Was your experience connecting to the web and viewing the video illustrations acceptable? Explain.

   _____

   _____

5. On a scale of 1 to 10 (10 being the highest) how would you rate:

   a) the quality and usefulness of the session content? _____
   b) the responsiveness and interaction of those in your group? _____

6. To what degree did this course deepen your practical understanding of the truths it covered?

   ❏ Little   ❏ Somewhat   ❏ Rather considerably

   Please give any comments you feel would be helpful to us.

   _____

   _____

   _____

   _____

Please mail to: Josh McDowell Evaluation
                 PO Box 4126
                 Copley, OH 44321

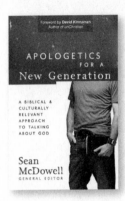

Apologetics for a New Generation
A Biblical and Culturally Relevant Approach to
Talking About God
Sean McDowell

This generation's faith is constantly under
attack from the secular media, skeptical teach-
ers, and unbelieving peers. You may wonder,
How can I help?

Working with young adults every day, Sean McDowell understands
their situation and shares your concern. His first-rate team of con-
tributors shows how you can help members of the new generation
plant their feet firmly on the truth. Find out how you can walk them
through the process of...

- formulating a biblical worldview and applying scriptural
  principles to everyday issues

- articulating their questions and addressing their doubts
  in a safe environment

- becoming confident in their faith and effective in their
  witness

The truth never gets old, but people need to hear it in fresh, new
ways. Find out how you can effectively share the answers to life's big
questions with a new generation.

The Awesome Book of Bible Answers for Kids

Josh McDowell and Kevin Johnson

These concise, welcoming answers include key Bible verses and explorations of topics that matter most to kids ages 8 to 12: God's love; right and wrong; Jesus, the Holy Spirit, and God's Word; different beliefs and religions; church, prayer, and sharing faith. Josh and Kevin look at questions like…

- How do I know God wants to be my friend?

- Are parts of the Bible make-believe, or is everything true?

- Was Jesus a wimp?

- Why do some Christians not act like Christians?

- Can God make bad things turn out okay?

The next time a child in your life asks a good question, this practical and engaging volume will give you helpful tips and conversation ideas so you can connect with them and offer straight talk about faith in Jesus. *Includes an easy-to-use learning and conversation guide.*

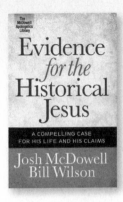

Evidence for the Historical Jesus
A Compelling Case for His Life and His Claims
Josh McDowell and Bill Wilson

After two years of intensive research, the agnostic Josh McDowell was convinced of the reliability of the historical evidence showing that Jesus of Nazareth existed and was precisely who he said he was—God in the flesh. Confronted by the living Lord, Josh accepted the offer of a relationship with him.

In *Evidence for the Historical Jesus,* Josh teams with writer-researcher Bill Wilson to provide you with a thorough analysis to document that Jesus Christ actually walked on this earth—and that the New Testament accounts are incredibly reliable in describing his life. The authors' broad-ranging investigation examines

- the writings of ancient rabbis, martyrs, and early church leaders

- the evidence of the New Testament text

- historical geography and archaeology

Detailed and incisive but accessible, this volume will help you relate to people who distort or discount Christianity and its Founder. And it will strengthen your confidence in Jesus Christ and in the Scriptures that document his words, his life, and his love.

The Unshakable Truth® church and small group resource collections are part of a unique collaboration between Harvest House Publishers and the Great Commandment Network. The Great Commandment Network is an international network of denominational partners, churches, parachurch ministries and strategic ministry leaders who are committed to the development of ongoing Great Commandment ministries worldwide as they prioritize the powerful simplicity of loving God, loving others and making disciples.

Through accredited trainers, the Great Commandment Network equips churches for ongoing relational ministry utilizing resources from the GC² Experience collection.

The GC² Experience Vision

To provide process-driven resources for a lifelong journey of spiritual formation. Every resource includes intentional opportunities to live out life-changing content within the context of loving God, loving others, and making disciples (Matthew 22:37-40; 28:19-20).

The GC² Experience Process includes:

- Experiential and transformative content. People are relationally transformed when they encounter Jesus, experience his Word, and engage in authentic community.
- Opportunities to move through a journey of…

  - Exploring Truth in the safety of relationship
  - Embracing Truth in a personal way
  - Experiencing Truth in everyday life
  - Expressing Truth through my identity as a Christ-follower

"Most of us have attended too many meetings and have gone through too many courses, only to conclude: We're leaving unchanged, and the people in our lives can see that we're unchanged. It is time to trust God for something different…a movement of life-changing transformation!"

Dr. David Ferguson
The Great Commandment Network

**The Transforming Promise of
Great Commandment/Great Commission Living**
www.GC2experience.com